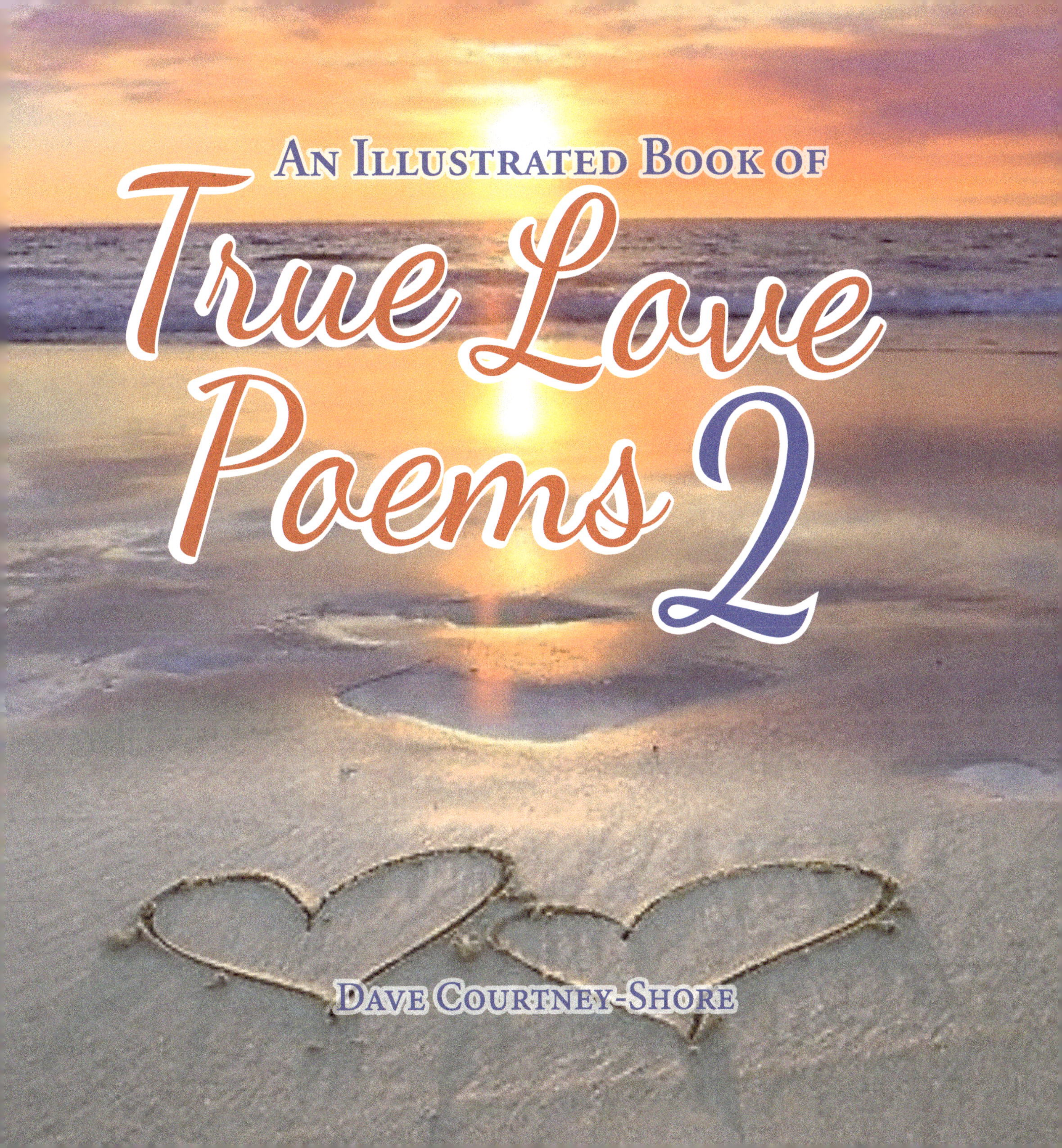

An Illustrated Book of

True Love Poems 2

Dave Courtney-Shore

Book Review

My poem man! In this 2nd book of illustrated love poems, I think Dave has come to love me even more, which Is difficult to believe if you read the first enthralling book of illustrated Love Poems!

Also, I cannot believe how fast he writes, and with such depth of feeling and a burning passion that just flows across each page, you simply cannot put the book down till the very end.

One cannot but feel and enjoy each poem for its loving and treasured moments, its insights into love situations that will make you grin or bear. True, heartfelt, and sincere, the poems at times seem to come from his soul. Also, many of the poems engender a good feel factor which will no doubt make you smile, if not hide a cheeky grin, as one reads on.

Written while landlocked on different continents miles apart, he still managed to continue to write from his heart. I think it kept him going through the Covid pandemic and somehow deepened the love that we found. I hope it does the same for you.

In his books, you will find love, joy and humour to enjoy and share. In this book, in particular, you will sense a growing love, which gets deeper, sexier and funnier as it progresses, until the very end where you end up dancing on the ceiling. - Mei Liu

ISBN: 978-1-64314-722-2 (Paperback)
978-1-64314-723-9 (Hardback)
978-1-64314-724-6 (E-book)

AUTHORS PRESS

AuthorsPress
California, USA
www.authorspress.com

I dedicate this second book to all those in love

And especially the one that I love.

I am yours and you are mine

You captured my heart

for all time.

Contents

ROMANCE

When we First Met

I met her in a bar in downtown Juffair
Ignored her till I locked onto her eyes which were on fire
Completely hooked and with no resistance to her charms
She took me away and I fell into her arms.

She then kissed me like no-one ever had
Took my body like I was a young lad!
She made love to me and I responded in kind
With strength and passion so hot and divine
Going on and on
Until she captured my very soul and then my heart
Never ever to be apart.

When I left, I wondered alone in a desert where I was bound
And questioned the love I had dearly found
She later reassured me and I forgot all my fears
Showed me the way which brought me to tears.

She has taken me to a place I would never have found
She has shown forgiveness, tenderness and love in bounds
I will love her forever how silly that may sound.

We will be together forever
For we care....
About enjoying the love we undoubtedly share.

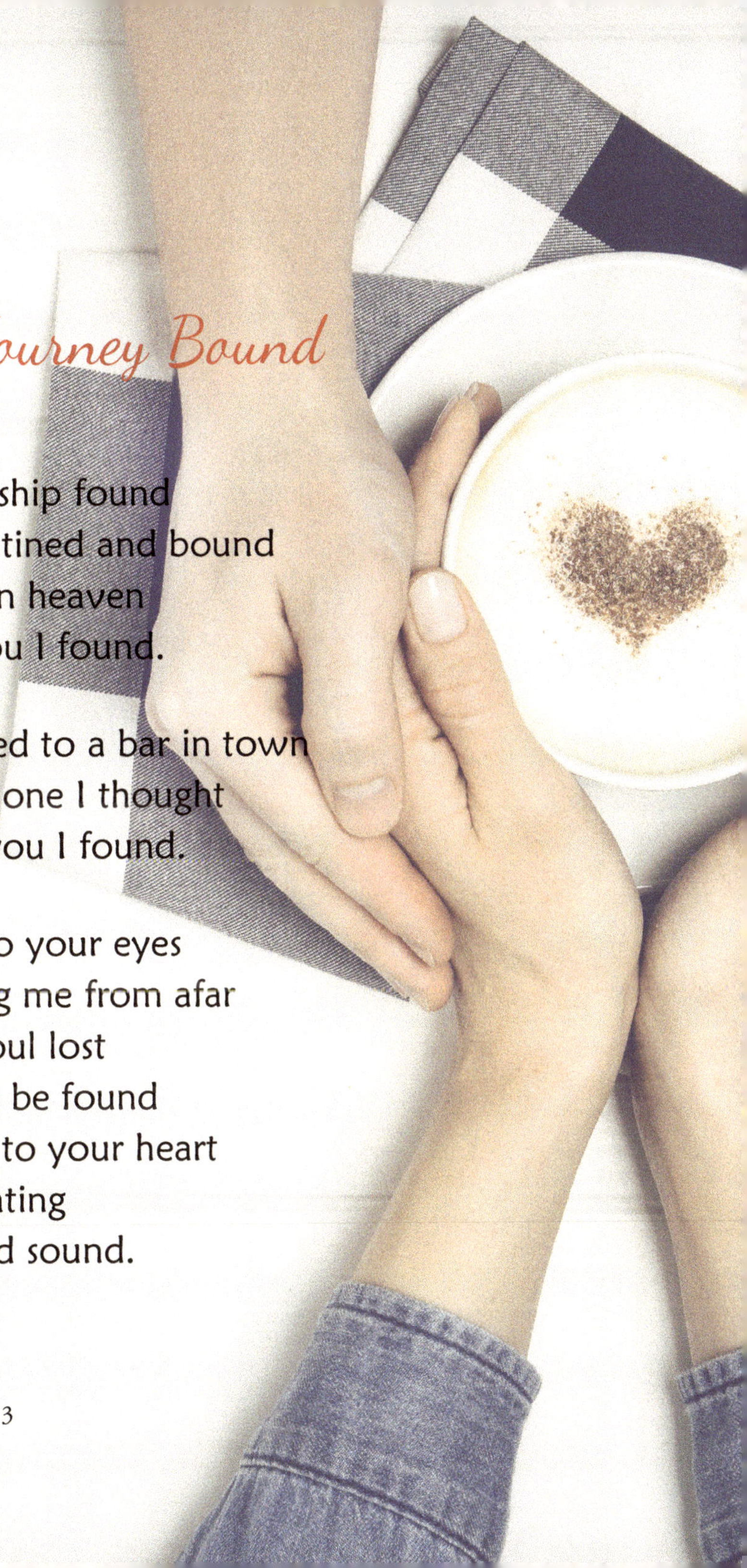

Life's Love Journey Bound

A relationship found
Unforgiving, destined and bound
Forged in heaven
Where you I found.

An Angel descended to a bar in town
Not wanting one I thought
But there you I found.

A look into your eyes
A voice calling me from afar
My soul lost
Never to be found
Except close to your heart
Beating
Safe and sound.

You led me from a lonely place
Saved my soul
Gave me destiny
And forgiveness with your grace.

It's been a long journey I know
But with you there is no other road
We travel together
Sometime in spirit, a back pack and a heavy load.

With you, together
Nothing to stop us on our way
Destined to be together
Whatever challenges found
We will reach there
Someday
Safe and sound.

Ode to a Princess of Love and Grace

You are my life
You are special
Yes a Princess and an Angel
A guiding light
Unknown but true.

Above all you stand so small but yet so tall
Your radiance not seen
But known in the hearts
Of many you meet
Left breathless in the person you have become
And whom you greet.

Everything is calm
Where you walk
Blessed are they
As is you
From your head to your feet.

Always loving, and patient
True to heart and soul
No one else have I ever met
So in the moment, so true
Even when times seem dark and blue
You are there
Ever true.

So, ever in the moment
Patient, wise
And stunning in every way
You walk in beauty
And so much grace
Love surrounds you
It can only be you.

Yes, it's true.

In the Glimpse of an Eye

Your eyes shine so brightly
Like stars in the sky
My heart in yours
It will never die
From heaven you come
In God's will you were made
In an Angels wings you were borne to me.

You simply put every other person in the shade.

It's Love

It's the look in their eye
The smile on their face
The nonchalant flick of the hair
Revealing a bare neckline and chest.

Their loving ways
With both passion and care
A gentle touch here
And a kiss over there.

A giggle that floats endlessly born on the air
A body that wiggles so sexy when bare
A body of beauty,
Born of charm and grace
No other can be found
In no other place.

You Make Me Happy

You make me happy
When I'm down 'n blue
Come rain or shine
I love you.

Be My Valentine

I love you now and for all time
I can't live without you
Be without you

Come, be with me
Make me happy
Please be mine.

A Thousand Years (Alternative Version)

I have waited for you for a1000 years
All that time holding back the fear and tears
Forever living out the message in this song
Even though for me it's been too long.

A song I thought I would never understand
But with you in joy I have now found
Forever I hope true love abounds.
Love between us ongoing, solid and sound.

I have loved you for a thousand years
And I will love you for another 1000 years
A journey with no bounds
Your love for me and my love for you
I truly believe we have found.

Now forever in each other's hearts,
Regularly beating, never apart.

Love and sharing kindness, caring and charm
We will be together in each other's arms.

You Were Sent To Me

You were sent to me from heaven
To be placed in my care
And me in yours
Nothing assumed or taken
All simply given
With nothing to spare.

I nearly killed you
But you saved mine
Then, now, until the end of time
Watching my back, treading my path
Holding my hand, when it gets dark.

Holding me up
When I've fallen down, in isolation and deep despair
When it seems, my life is at its end and beyond repair.

Keeping me warm
When I feel lonely and cold
Keeping me steadfast on what appears a long bleak road.

Leading me ultimately
To a place I want to be
Blessed in love,
Peace and Sanctity.

Where I will look after you
And you will look after me.

TRUE LOVE

Let's Get It Together

Without you I would not exist
As my problems and pain still persist
Help me make it through the pain
Let me live my life again
Let's be together for all time
Come be with me come rain or shine.

You're in my heart,
But the World is against me
Grinding me down
Making me miserable
Tearing me apart.

If I we can't shake it,
Break it or make it
I will surely perish
As I can't afford to lose
The only thing I cherish.

I'm a survivor
But I need you now
I can't wait forever
So, let's make it happen
Let's get it on
Let's get it together.

True Love

True love has no bounds
Nothing can get in its way
Because when you are both truly in love
There's nothing can stop you
Nothing anyone can say.

True Love So

Oh so true
True love with you, only you
There can be no better
Than the love we have for each other.

Never ending, always sending
What we know is true
Our heartfelt love, care and devotion
Putting in motion
What is clearly meant for me and you.

Undying love that binds us
It's kind of us I guess
Just beginning but never ending
I guess it's true. .

I Love You

I love you
I see it in films
Of love and sadness
I know you
I will never let you go
As you know.

I will love you forever
Never let you go
I will follow you
Wherever you want to go.

And we will be together
Come what may
We will strive to be together
Its destiny
And so much more
We will join together
On a distant shore.

It's the lore
Yes the World is ours
Of that I'm sure.

For us to treasure
To share and be as one
Always together
All for one
Never alone
Sharing love
Yes on that distant shore
Yes of that I am sure.

Always.

When I'm With You

When I see your face
I see the Universe opening up for me
In all its glory and grace
Everything is bright
As beautiful as you
As wonderful as can be.

A Time and a Place called Love

There is a Time and a Place for us
Somewhere unknown but very close
I will take you there if you dare
Just hold my hand
Fly with me beyond the stars
To a place called love.

We must go there soon
As no-one will wait for us
A paradise awaits
Not a moment to lose
Our fate, yours and mine.

Somewhere close but not in this time
While we may tip toe through this life
We will boldly step into another
Beyond this realm beyond this time.
Come with me
Into the future, infinite time
Love and joy unbound
There for us to find.

On a lighter note.....

Love Bun

Now and evermore, never doubted, always sure
Loving, living, laughing, having fun
Yep, that's me and you, love bun.

Eternal Love

For All Eternity

For all eternity
Through time and space
We will travel together
Sharing our love
With nothing to hide.

Love lasting forever
We will be together
For all time.

Everything to live for
Everything to love for
Everything to see and enjoy
All there across the Universe
For me and you to find.

A Place Frozen in Time

There is a place frozen in time
Waiting for me, and what is mine
I know where it is
I see it in a rhyme.

A place that sings in nature
Cool fresh as mountain dew
In a forest clearing
There waiting for me and you.

The trees dancing in the breeze
Grass up to your knees
Brook whispering in your ears
Leaves rustling in the wind.

Birds shaking their feathers in a spring
Logs bobbing downstream
Sun glinting through the trees
All shining on you and me.

A Time and a Place

There is a Time and a Place for us
Somewhere unknown but very close
I will take you there, if you dare
Just hold my hand
Fly with me without a care
Above the stars
To a place called love.

We must go there soon
As no-one will wait for us
A paradise awaits
Not a moment to lose
Our fate, yours and mine
In which we must trust.

Somewhere close, but not in this time
While we may tip toe through this life
We will boldly step into another
Beyond this realm beyond this time.

Come with me
Into the future, infinite time
Love and joy unbound
There for us to find.

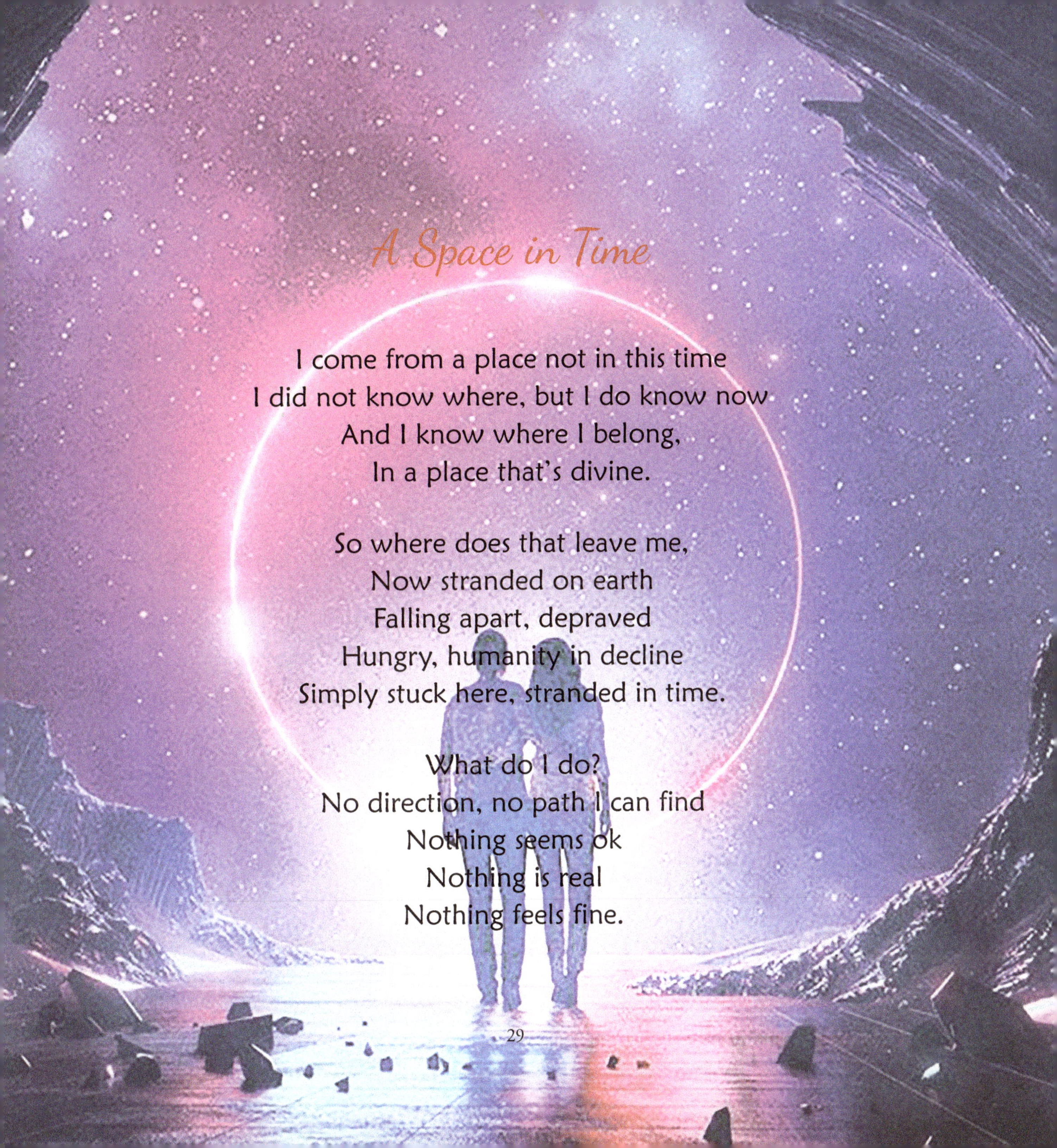

A Space in Time

I come from a place not in this time
I did not know where, but I do know now
And I know where I belong,
In a place that's divine.

So where does that leave me,
Now stranded on earth
Falling apart, depraved
Hungry, humanity in decline
Simply stuck here, stranded in time.

What do I do?
No direction, no path I can find
Nothing seems ok
Nothing is real
Nothing feels fine.

I'm alone, lonely
All I have is mine
What is that worth?
Nothing
Just ain't worth a dime.

Can't even take it with me
As I travel through space in time
On an adventure that is about to begin
Seems weird, wonderful, maybe worrying
And yet somewhat sublime.

Am I prepared?
Hell No?
But should I be?
Should I be motivated to get up and go
To wander the universe
With just me and mine?
I could go on my own
But what purpose does that serve?
No-one to share the adventure with
To see the wonders beyond this earth,
Beyond this parallel universe
Through this future tunnel in time.

On a journey across the stars
To worlds' unknown
New life forms
New wonders, sensations, feelings
That surely must be shared.

Will you join me beyond the stars?
Beyond the Moon we will travel far
Blinking as we pass Mars
Turning around Venus, as the Sun rises and flares
Flying past Neptune and beyond the Galaxy
Into a dark mass of no return
We venture forward come what may
Unknown, sometimes bleak and gray.

Then immersing ourselves in the light
and starry sky and mist of the Milky Way.
Naked and free
Wide-eyed and fancy-free
Yes that could be you and me.

As we Journey on
through the Cosmos flowing,
spiraling out of control.

Around you and me
Bound together entwined in love forever
Searched and found
Making love in harmony with the Universe
Truly earned and yet duty-bound
It's there for us to take
It has to be.

I Must be There

It's there
I hear it on the solar wind
From a beach on a lonely deserted distant shore
Pristine, pure and clean
Palm trees swaying in a gentle wind
Surf sparkling on the sand
Spreading its wing.

On a sandy beach
Pressing sand on light pretty feet
It's just made for you and me
And those with a kindred spirit,
together
In total joy, peace and harmony.

My Shining Star

A love that transverses the Universe
Never to be questioned
Rarely found
Never broken
Onward bound.

Together forever
Through this earthly experience and beyond
We journey together
Through eternity and beyond.

Beyond the Galaxy and the Milky Way
At warp speed, zero mass and gravity
Leading the way
To another life
Another Galaxy.

As we travel to distant shores
I'm you're Mars
You're my Venus
My little shining star.

Through Clouds of Cosmic Gas
Asteroids and Comets
Spinning planets
Circling moons and
distant Blue Horizons
Supernovas, Black Holes and the Milky Way
I will be with you
Come what may.

Super Heroes

You are my Supergirl
My Florence Nightingale
My Mary Magdalene
My Meryl Streep
My Rapunzel in a Castle Keep.

I am your Romeo, you are my Juliet
I am your Aramis, you are my French Queen
I'm your Brad Pitt, you are my Jolene.

I am your Superman, you are Lois lane
I am Tarzan, you Jane.
You are all of them
And I'm James Dean.

Above All

You are my Empress, Princess and my Queen
So gentle, honest, pure and clean.

Many characters to embrace,
Adventures to have
Enjoying the race
Through endless time
Just remember this
I will always be yours
And you will always be mine.

Endless bliss, just give me a kiss!

Being Apart

I miss you so much.
Not there to touch
One day
I will be there
Holding you close to me
Never again to part.

I am Yours

You playing with me, kissing, teasing me too
Me slipping and falling in love with you
Sometimes happy, sometimes blue
Yet my love for you always true
I hope you need me as I need you.

Birds of Paradise in Flight

When you are around the birds of paradise are everywhere to be seen
You only need to look over the balcony as the sun goes down
To see a couple of love birds chirping in the trees
Expressing their love for each other
As I do for thee.

And as you take flight and leave this shore
I stand alone in the breeze somewhat cold and unsure
I can only hold onto the love we shared
Special moments, here and there.
As I listen to birds in flight
Wishing I was there.

I patiently wait for the dawn of the day
When we will be together again
Come what may.

Now I See You Clearly

Now I see you clearly
Love grows and knows no bounds
Like waves rolling from the sea
Never ceasing, ever reaching
Bringing you closer to me.

I was blind
Lost and found
Your amazing grace
Makes my heart sing
With joy and peace
At every sound.

Holding Out For You

Our life will be great
Whatever we have to go through
As there is so much to live for and revive
So much we have already gone through,
And still we love each other
And still we survive.

I know my destiny is with you
There is no other
I want to be with, but you
You are my heart and soul
My reason to survive
So let it be, and make it so.

Nothing is impossible, when I am with you
You bring me hope and life
Amidst all this travesty and strife
My heart yearns for you

I won't give you up.
I will be with you
Just wait and see.

I will be true and be with you
Whatever it takes
I will not break
Whatever the heart ache
I will hold out for you.

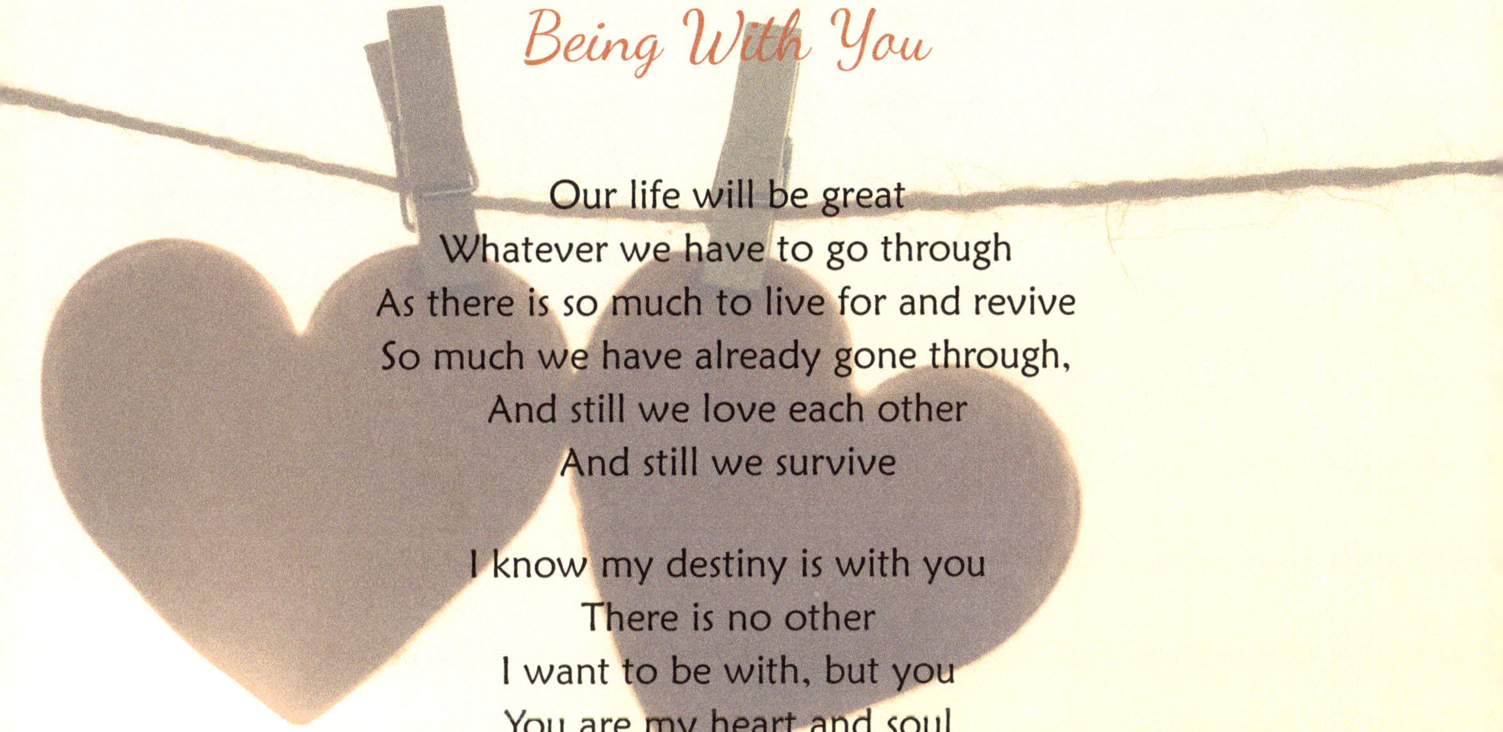

Being With You

Our life will be great
Whatever we have to go through
As there is so much to live for and revive
So much we have already gone through,
And still we love each other
And still we survive

I know my destiny is with you
There is no other
I want to be with, but you
You are my heart and soul
My reason to survive
So let it be, and make it so.

Nothing is impossible, when I am with you
You bring me hope and life
Amidst all this travesty and strife
My heart yearns for you
I won't give you up
I will be with you
Just wait and see.

I will be true and be with you
Whatever it takes
I will not break
Whatever the heart ache
I will hold out for you.

Meaning To My Life

I can't believe it really
You have brought meaning to my life
Challenging sometimes
But I believe and truly love you
I will always be by your side.

A Gift

We both have a gift
We need to share
To be together
For us to enjoy
Whatever we feel
Whatever the weather.

It's up to us
To make this happen
We need each other
More now than ever.

Love is Not Old

We will not leave or live without each other
I hope we will always be happy
As you're everything to me
And I love you forever.

Never to Forget

Nothing ever will ever be the same again
Since I met and fell in love with you
You're the smile on my face
The lift in my step
My reason for living and giving
Bringing life to meaning
Never ever to forget.

I will love you forever
Every step we take.

Anywhere Will Do

Anywhere

The warmth the smell of you...
Awakens my loins
I can't resist you, want you all the time
Want to be and come with you
Anywhere–will just be fine!

Love on the Beach

Awake the dawn
On a bright new day
Feel our love rise
And fill the bay.

Holding hands
Walking in the sand
Sea at our feet
Hearts skipping a beat.

Sun on our shoulders
Wind in our hair
Feeling the breeze
Of the cool morning air.

In the buff, in the rough
Innocent, naked and bare
Let's kiss, make love, doing what we like, Without a care.

Fun in the Foam

The spark in your eyes
Your hair floating in the night air
Your head on my shoulder, cold and bare
Your eyes holding that heavenly stare
As we stroll along the beach
Without a care.

Your arms encircling my waist
Your body moving with such sweetness and grace
Your hands in harmony with mine
As our bodies draw closer and entwine
Feeling the pleasure, feeling the heat
Feeling the desire
In your hot embrace.

Your lips wet and moist
Tongue seeking mine
Drawing me deeper
Taking me down
Holding me firm
Taking me in
Thrusting, heaving
Occasionally breathing
At every twist and turn.

Ain't no stopping
Buried deep
I feel it baby, feel it burning
Feel the glow,
As I reach along the beach
For the very depths of your soul.

Take me baby
Take me to your pleasure dome
Where I can play
Now and every day
Happy and contented
In the sand washed foam.

Under the Stars

As we walk hand in hand
Leaving footprints in the sand
Feeling the breeze coming off the sea
Watching the sun set over you and me.

The moon rising to light our way
Stars twinkling in the Milky Way
Consternations appearing in the glare
Planets passing here and there.

The Universe for us all to see
But on a deserted beach,
There is only you and me
Making love in harmony,
Under the Stars,
The Universe,
And the Galaxy.

The Knight

I awake as a knight from the dark depths of the night
I'm ready for battle and rally for the fight.

Quickly donning my armour and raising my sword
I hear it sing and ring again
And like birds on the wing
I hear the call.

Riding high and aloft in the breeze that beck-
ons on the back of the breaking dawn
It shines and glistens in the dew and glow
of the sun in the morning dawn
It points me like a torch and a beacon of light
That rises in the east', and settles in the West
Where I must make my stand and fight
To fight for what is right.

Across a land that is worth fighting for
I thrust it against my chest with a rhythm that matches my beating heart
And with fire in my belly
And a burning desire
that rages in my chest
I journey on a mission and a long-lost quest
To rescue the one I hear they call
The damsel in distress.

And a story to be told
Sleeping deep in my very soul.

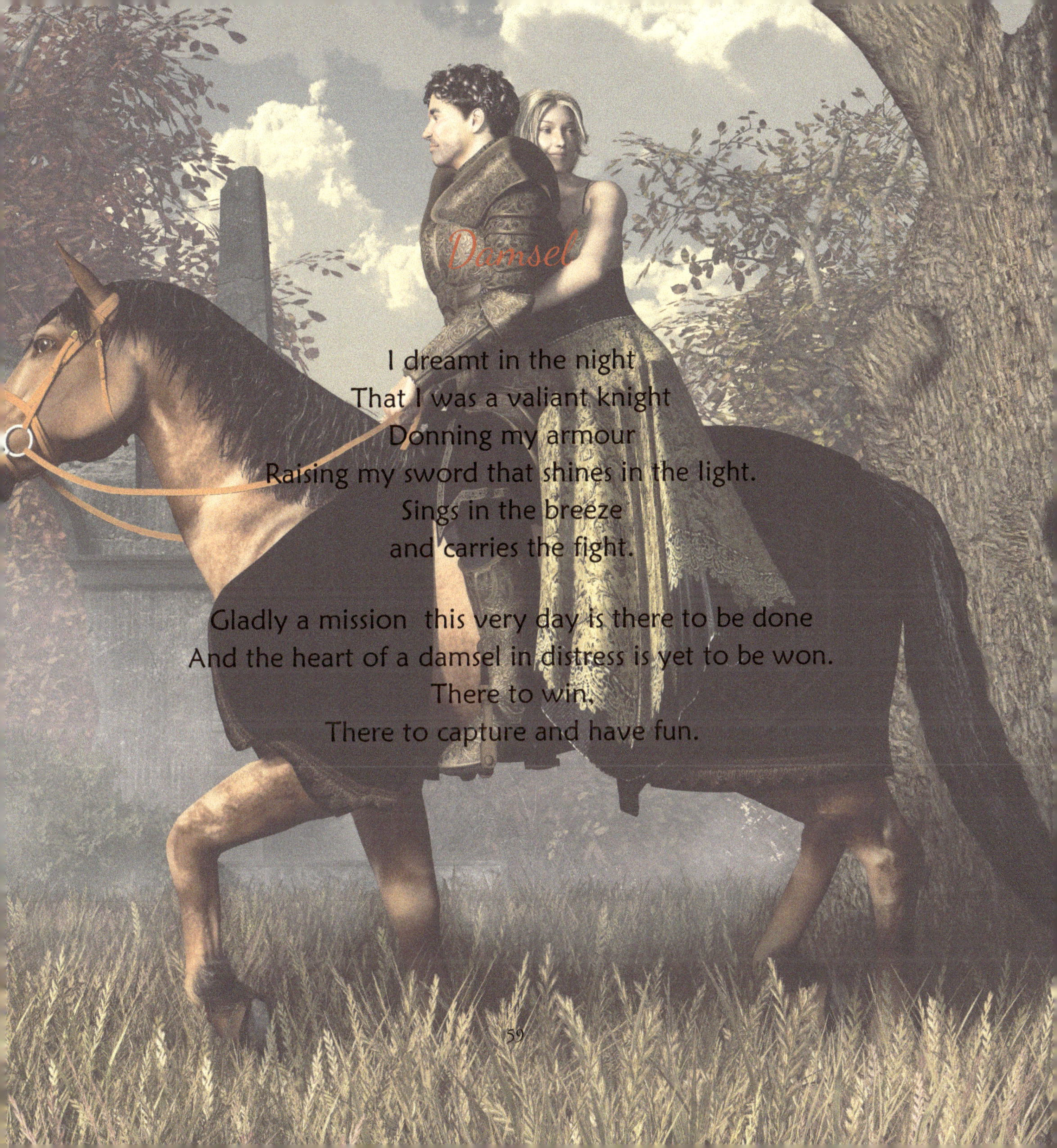

Damsel

I dreamt in the night
That I was a valiant knight
Donning my armour
Raising my sword that shines in the light.
Sings in the breeze
and carries the fight.

Gladly a mission this very day is there to be done
And the heart of a damsel in distress is yet to be won.
There to win,
There to capture and have fun.

Sex

Can't stop what nature set out for us
Let's do it straight up
Make no fuss
Don't fake it
Have fun
Till all is spent and we are done.

Lust

The dawn breaks and you awake
Reaching over me in bed to kiss and make
Your hand slides down my body to find that I'm ready and awake
My legs open wide as my groin begins to ache
You hold my passion in your hands
I cannot speak
I am yours and you are mine to take.

Your eyes widen to the touch
You moisten in places that cannot as yet be reached but must
We feel each other's lust
Rise in each other's hold
Desire breaks it's too much to resist and behold
We must take of each other's pleasure while it still exists and unfolds
To heights that soar and peak above the caverns
Of which we whisper and speak as in heaven
That must reveal themselves
And be taken

The Sun Shines Through Your Hair

The Sun shines through your hair
Oh! to be so gorgeous and one so fair
On such a bright beautiful day
As beautiful as you
As you walk through fields of golden hay
There with you I wish to be
There I will take you
Make love to you
If I may.

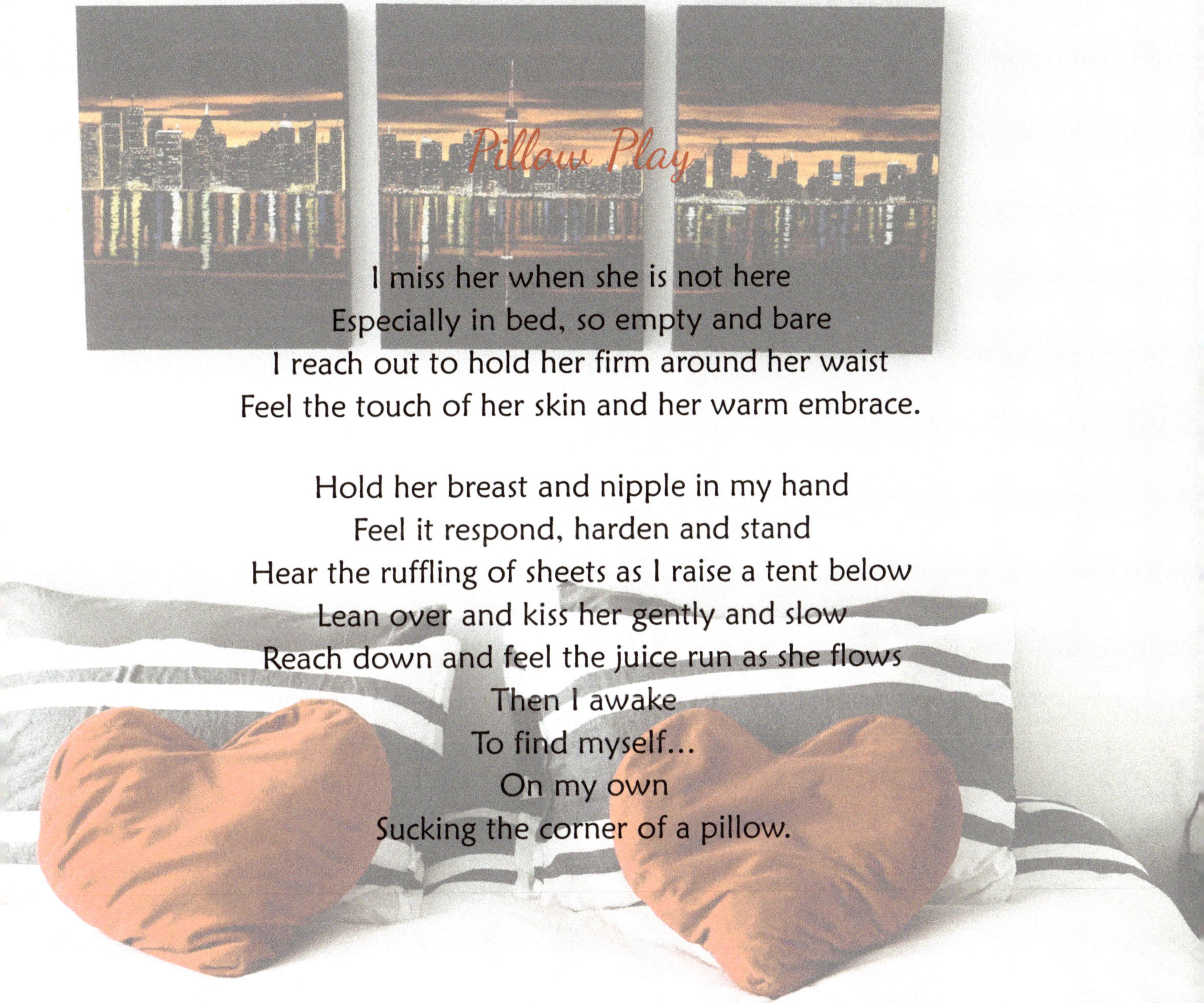

Pillow Play

I miss her when she is not here
Especially in bed, so empty and bare
I reach out to hold her firm around her waist
Feel the touch of her skin and her warm embrace.

Hold her breast and nipple in my hand
Feel it respond, harden and stand
Hear the ruffling of sheets as I raise a tent below
Lean over and kiss her gently and slow
Reach down and feel the juice run as she flows
Then I awake
To find myself…
On my own
Sucking the corner of a pillow.

Ted!

I awake in the night
And you are not there
Another night I cannot bare…
Ted looks at me with a cross–eyed stare
But I need **you** now to be with **me**
To make love with you and kick out the bear!

Come With Me

Please come lie beside me
Hold me firm, take and guide me
Raise me up and hold me tight
Kiss and love me through this night

Hold yourself as if it matters
While your legs are spread across the mattress
Nipples bruised and hard with pleasure
Lips swollen with kissing and constant pressure.

Let me love you like you've never known
Bite your lip between the groans
Beg me never to stop
Hold the bed head while it rocks
Whilst I remove your ruffled frock
And make love to you
Firm stiff and hard as a rock.

Pleasure Dome

The spark in your eyes
Your hair floating in the night air
Your head on my shoulder bare
Your eyes holding a heavenly stare
As we stroll along the beach
Without a care.

Your arms encircling my waist
Your body moving with such sweetness and grace
Your hands in harmony with mine
As our bodies draw closer and entwine
Feeling the pleasure, feeling the heat
Feeling the desire
In your hot embrace

Your lips wet and moist
Tongue seeking mine
Drawing me deeper
Drawing me down
Holding me firm
Lighting my fire
Feeling the burn.

Ain't no holding me now
Thrusting
Heaving
Heavy breathing.

Ain't no stopping me now, babe
Buried deep
Feel it baby
Feel it burning,
Down to the very depths of your soul.

Take me baby
Take me home
Take me to your pleasure dome.

Heaven

Take me to heavenly depths beyond compare
Beyond the horizon where no woman dares
Show me the place where I can dive
To live, love and feel the depth of my heart's desire.

Time for a Pee?

You're body close to mine
Your hand holding mine
Our eyes closed in time
Our bodies reaching for each other
Ready to entwine, but
Oh No,
It's time for pee-pee.

Lost in Love—Angels in Arms

I often cry
I don't know why
I'm lost in love
Leaving one who nearly destroyed me
To find another who abuses me
Time after time.

Whenever will I learn maybe never before I die
But I have a heart and an angel by my side
She is sat beside me now
Telling me I am moral and strong
I live the future
Someday strong
Living happy contented and just fine.

I know the angels are with me now
Laughing shouting my song
I know now I will not come to harm
As we will all be angels in arms sometime.

Song n Dance

Dancing to the Rhythm

Roll it up
Rock it down
Move to the rhythm
Don't let your feet
Touch the ground.

Shuffle your feet
To the sound and the beat
Shake your body
Feel the heat.

Do it baby
One more time
Roll your eyes and turn around
Hit me with your
"I want you" stare
Come to me if you dare.

Move slowly with me to the pulsating beat
Feel your body shake right down to your feet
Come with me, let's ride high
Come with me
And touch the sky.

Strip me naked
Raw and bare
Hold me close
While I take you there.

Take me now
Wait no more
Take me to a place
I've never been before.

Rock me gently
Rock me sweet
Take me again
Knock me off my feet.

Raise me up
Hold me down
Find the place
Where you take
my crown.

Roll me over
Slide across the floor
Meet me again
Open my door
Rock me again
Till I can't take
any more.

Dance the Night Away

It would be great to see you and dance the night away,
Somewhere with loads of people and friends
Somewhere we could run and play.

On a beach, remote but music blasting from god knows where

The moon and stars above as we dance in the glare

Until we sleep where we drop

And suck in the damp sea air.

To rise as the sun awakens us in the dawn

Time to make love again, refreshed, reborn

Make rhythm, and move to the pulsing beat

Feel the sand and sea squirm in our feet
Shed our clothes

Hit the beach.

And heh, have more fun

Burning our bums

In the morning Sun.

Chicken Shack – Move it on up

Move your body baby
And never look back
Cos I'm the Rooster
And there ain't no slack
So, come with me
And play away
In my funky little ole' Chicken Shack.

Feel the heat baby
Move it on up
Raise the sound
Feel the blast
An don't hold it down
Just feel the funky rhythm
And listen to the beat.
Break a sweat baby

And just soak it up
Feel the heat rising
Through your tiny little feet.

Rock and Reel
Weave and Wind
Shake and Shuffle
Gyrate and Grind.

Move it on up baby
You're doing fine
Turn it up
Sweet Music Mine.

Move it on up
To the rhythm and the beat
Shake it up baby
Let's feel the heat.

Let's get it together
Let's feel the grind
Cos baby you're coming with me
You're all mine.

Feel the rhythm
Shuffle your feet
Move your body
And swing to the beat.

Hold me close
As if naked and bare
Move it on up baby
You're almost there.

Move it on up baby
To the rhythm and the beat
Hold that feeling
Rocking and reeling
Let's go make love
On the f...... ceiling.

So, don't relax
Don't hold back
Till we finally make it
And break the roof
On my little ole' Chicken Shack.

About the Author

Dave was born and grew up on the shores of England and following his schooling travelled around the World working for consultancies and institutions like PWC, the World Bank and United Nations, in some of the richest and indeed poorest places on the planet. Besides troubleshooting projects, sometimes in the middle of nowhere, sometimes left on his own, he learned much about people and life, its challenges and experiences, some deep and profound.

His love of poetry really came to life when he fell in love, not for the first time but this time for real. Such experiences are shared in his trilogy of books entitled "Illustrated Book of True Love Poems" of which this is the second.

Raw, sometimes brutally honest, sometimes funny, but always from the heart, exploring what is meant by love and a relationship that still stands on solid ground, and yet has no bounds.

Written by Dave Courtney-Shore

Should you like to have a poem written for yourself
or a loved one please contact me at:

davecourtneyshore@gmail.com

US Review of Books

in partnership with AUTHORSPRESS

AN ILLUSTRATED BOOK OF

True Love Poems 2

by Dave Courtney-Shore

book review by R.J. Johnson

THE US Review of Books

AUTHORS PRESS

CREATIVE BOOKS

For readers who like poetry that inspires a reader to "grin or bear," this is a fun collection to add to the shelf.

—**R.J. Johnson**
The US Review of Books

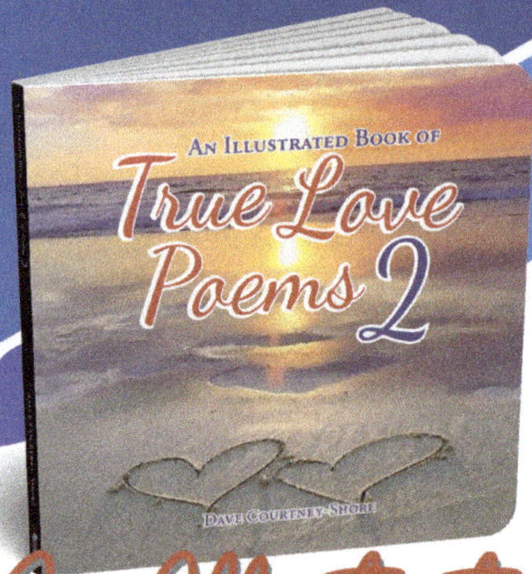

An Illustrated Book of True Love Poems 2

by Dave Courtney-Shore

"She has taken me to a place I would have never found."

This is a collection of love poetry that expresses longing, devotion, promise, and lighthearted companionship. Peaceful and hopeful images accompany the poems. The book is a festival of lyrical play and visual pleasures, making it a perfect sentimental gift for lovers to read together. The poems explore a variety of themes. The straightforward poetry could also encourage lovers on special occasions, such as Valentine's Day, a wedding day, an anniversary, or through a courtship.

Love poetry has a long tradition extending back to Sappho, etc. These poems might give someone who doesn't have experience with poetry a sense of confidence and energy to express their true love. The words capture the spirit of longing and the promise of undying love. The verses convey familiar sentiments that can give the reader warm reassurance. Just knowing such love exists in this wary world fills the heart with strength.

The US Review of Books

AUTHORS PRESS

CREATIVE BOOKS

ne lover offers the poetry to the beloved. Any sense of repetition signals dedication to the love of one's life. Some the accompanying photographs have people in them, while others have more abstract designs. Some images e serene scenes, such as a beach. The photos convey some of the sentiments of the poetry.

hat's unique and compelling about this collection is how it moves through various moods of the poet. For kample, there is a yearning and longing mood and a steadfast and committed one. There is a lustful mood as well s a mood of companionship and fun. All these moods in one collection help affirm the spectrum of emotions that ccompanies being in love. A line from the poem "My Shining Star" expresses bold confidence: "A love that ansverses the universe / never to be questioned / rarely found / never broken / onward bound." The image ccompanying the poem reveals a twilight sky with stars shining around the words that invoke sentiments of eace and infinity. Even if lovers are apart and cannot travel to see each other in person, the lover's longing offers n unbreakable promise and undying hope that they will be together again.

wo more themes inspire strength: love is eternal, and there's always hope that the beloved reciprocates the elings. "Nothing is impossible when I am with you / You bring me hope and life / Amidst all this travesty and strife My heart yearns for you." Striking a lighter tone, some poems contain cheerful erotic suggestions: "In the buff, in ne rough / Innocent, naked and bare / Let's kiss, make love, doing what we like, Without a care." Perhaps the reader ill wonder why the "W" in the last phrase is capitalized, but maybe this is the point. The poet may be emphasizing Without" a care because the lover's intimacy knows that he and his beloved are the only two people in the world.

ther selections stand out due to the feelings they foster. For instance, there is a sentiment of chivalry with an nage of a knight and his damsel on a horse. The poem is called "Damsel" and charms anyone who adores classic nivalry. Dichotomy is also present in the collection. Poems such as "Sex" and "Lust" communicate two consenting overs in the throes of passion. But then these are followed by "The Sun Shines Through Your Hair," which sounds nore like a fantasy, and the poet retreats to more longing as a reminder that the consummation of a relationship still negotiable. This feature makes the poetry collection feel colorful and dynamic.

n the book's introduction, the beloved Mei Liu writes, "One cannot but feel and enjoy each poem for its loving and easured moments, its insights into love situations that will make you grin or bear." For readers who like poetry that nspires a reader to "grin or bear," this is a fun collection to add to the shelf.

ook review by R.J. Johnson

CPSIA information can be obtained
at www.ICGtesting.com
Printed in the USA
LVHW070219140422
716182LV00008B/199

9 781643 147239